WORDS OF WISDOM

Encouraging Quotes from Inspiring Leaders

By Larry Bryant

WORDS OF WISDOM

Encouraging Quotes from Inspiring Leaders

By Larry Bryant

Printed by Amazon KDP
Created and published through the Publishing to Profit Training Quote Book
Generator

Printed in the United States of America
10 9 8 7 6 5 4 3 2

Introduction

Be encouraged and inspired by daily quotes. Begin by reading the quote in the morning and reflect on it throughout the day.

To Natasha, my wife, thank you for believing in me and inspiring me to follow my dreams.

"You are never to old to set another goal or to dream a new dream." -C. S. Lewis

Beginning Your Day

What does this quote mean to me personally today?

____

____

____

How will I apply this quote today?

____

____

____

Who else needs to hear this quote today?

____

____

____

At the End of Your Day

How did I apply this quote today?

____

____

____

What will I do differently going forward?

____

____

____

"Every adventure requires a first step. By now you realize this is it, your adventure awaits." -Larry Bryant

Beginning Your Day

What does this quote mean to me personally today?

____

____

How will I apply this quote today?

____

____

Who else needs to hear this quote today?

____

____

At the End of Your Day

How did I apply this quote today?

____

____

What will I do differently going forward?

____

____

"The most beautiful people are those who have known defeat, known suffering, known struggle, known loss, and have found their way out of the depths. These persons have an appreciation, sensitivity, and an understanding of life that fills them with compassion, gentleness, and a deep loving concern. Beautiful people do not just happen." -Elizabeth Kubler Ross

Beginning Your Day

What does this quote mean to me personally today?

____

____

____

How will I apply this quote today?

____

____

____

Who else needs to hear this quote today?

____

____

____

At the End of Your Day

How did I apply this quote today?

____

____

____

What will I do differently going forward?

____

____

____

"Be thankful for what you have; you'll end up having more. If you concentrate on what you don't have, you will never, ever have enough."
-Oprah Winfrey

Beginning Your Day
What does this quote mean to me personally today?

____

____

____

How will I apply this quote today?

____

____

____

Who else needs to hear this quote today?

____

____

____

At the End of Your Day
How did I apply this quote today?

____

____

____

What will I do differently going forward?

____

____

____

"Believe you can and you're half way there."
-Theodore Roosevelt

Beginning Your Day

What does this quote mean to me personally today?

____

____

____

How will I apply this quote today?

____

____

____

Who else needs to hear this quote today?

____

____

____

At the End of Your Day

How did I apply this quote today?

____

____

____

What will I do differently going forward?

____

____

____

"A goal without a date is just a dream." -Milton H. Erickson

Beginning Your Day

What does this quote mean to me personally today?

____

____

____

How will I apply this quote today?

____

____

____

Who else needs to hear this quote today?

____

____

____

At the End of Your Day

How did I apply this quote today?

____

____

____

What will I do differently going forward?

____

____

____

"You can never cross the ocean until you have the courage to lose sight of the shore." -Christopher Columbus

Beginning Your Day

What does this quote mean to me personally today?

____

____

____

How will I apply this quote today?

____

____

____

Who else needs to hear this quote today?

____

____

____

At the End of Your Day

How did I apply this quote today?

____

____

____

What will I do differently going forward?

____

____

____

"If it isn't making you better, it isn't love. True love makes you more of who you are, not less." -Mandy Hale

Beginning Your Day

What does this quote mean to me personally today?

____

____

____

How will I apply this quote today?

____

____

____

Who else needs to hear this quote today?

____

____

____

At the End of Your Day

How did I apply this quote today?

____

____

____

What will I do differently going forward?

____

____

____

"If you accept the expectations of others, especially negative ones, then you never will change the outcome." -Michael Jordan

Beginning Your Day

What does this quote mean to me personally today?

____

____

____

How will I apply this quote today?

____

____

____

Who else needs to hear this quote today?

____

____

____

At the End of Your Day

How did I apply this quote today?

____

____

____

What will I do differently going forward?

____

____

____

"If we did all the things we are capable of, we would literally astound ourselves." -Thomas A. Edison

Beginning Your Day

What does this quote mean to me personally today?

____

____

____

How will I apply this quote today?

____

____

____

Who else needs to hear this quote today?

____

____

____

At the End of Your Day

How did I apply this quote today?

____

____

____

What will I do differently going forward?

____

____

____

"The minute you start compromising for the sake of massaging somebody's ego, that's it, game over." -Gordon Ramsay

Beginning Your Day

What does this quote mean to me personally today?

____

____

____

How will I apply this quote today?

____

____

____

Who else needs to hear this quote today?

____

____

____

At the End of Your Day

How did I apply this quote today?

____

____

____

What will I do differently going forward?

____

____

____

"Why fit in when you were born to stand out?"
-Dr. Seuss

Beginning Your Day

What does this quote mean to me personally today?

____

____

____

How will I apply this quote today?

____

____

____

Who else needs to hear this quote today?

____

____

____

At the End of Your Day

How did I apply this quote today?

____

____

____

What will I do differently going forward?

____

____

"Our ambition should be to rule ourselves, the true kingdom for each one of us; and true progress is to know more, and be more, and to do more." -Oscar Wilde

Beginning Your Day

What does this quote mean to me personally today?

____

____

____

How will I apply this quote today?

____

____

____

Who else needs to hear this quote today?

____

____

At the End of Your Day

How did I apply this quote today?

____

____

What will I do differently going forward?

____

____

____

"You miss 100% of the shots you don't take."
-Wayne Gretzky

Beginning Your Day

What does this quote mean to me personally today?

____

____

How will I apply this quote today?

____

____

Who else needs to hear this quote today?

____

____

At the End of Your Day

How did I apply this quote today?

____

____

What will I do differently going forward?

____

____

"If you really want to do something, you will find a way. If you don't, you'll find an excuse." -Jim Rohn

Beginning Your Day

What does this quote mean to me personally today?

____

____

____

How will I apply this quote today?

____

____

____

Who else needs to hear this quote today?

____

____

____

At the End of Your Day

How did I apply this quote today?

____

____

____

What will I do differently going forward?

____

____

____

"I like nonsense, it wakes up the brain cells. Fantasy is a necessary ingredient in living, it's a way of looking at life through the wrong end of a telescope. Which is what I do, and that enables you to laugh at life's realities." -Dr. Seuss

Beginning Your Day

What does this quote mean to me personally today?

____

____

____

How will I apply this quote today?

____

____

____

Who else needs to hear this quote today?

____

____

____

At the End of Your Day

How did I apply this quote today?

____

____

____

What will I do differently going forward?

____

____

____

"Carry out a random act of kindness, with no expectation of reward, safe in the knowledge that one day someone might do the same for you." -Princess Diana

Beginning Your Day

What does this quote mean to me personally today?

____

____

____

How will I apply this quote today?

____

____

____

Who else needs to hear this quote today?

____

____

____

At the End of Your Day

How did I apply this quote today?

____

____

____

What will I do differently going forward?

____

____

____

"Success is not final, failure is not fatal; it is courage to continue that counts." -Winston Churchill

Beginning Your Day

What does this quote mean to me personally today?

____

____

____

How will I apply this quote today?

____

____

____

Who else needs to hear this quote today?

____

____

____

At the End of Your Day

How did I apply this quote today?

____

____

____

What will I do differently going forward?

____

____

____

"If you were born poor it's not your mistake, but if you die poor, it is your mistake." -Bill Gates

Beginning Your Day

What does this quote mean to me personally today?

____

____

____

How will I apply this quote today?

____

____

____

Who else needs to hear this quote today?

____

____

____

At the End of Your Day

How did I apply this quote today?

____

____

____

What will I do differently going forward?

____

____

____

"A seed planted in the ground does not feel its lack of roots, stem and petals as a 'weakness' or being 'less than'. It simply sees an opportunity to grow and then does." -Michael Stevenson

Beginning Your Day

What does this quote mean to me personally today?

____
____
____

How will I apply this quote today?

____
____
____

Who else needs to hear this quote today?

____
____
____

At the End of Your Day

How did I apply this quote today?

____
____
____

What will I do differently going forward?

____
____
____

"Defeat is a state of mind; no one is ever defeated until defeat has been accepted as a reality." -Bruce Lee

Beginning Your Day

What does this quote mean to me personally today?

____

____

____

How will I apply this quote today?

____

____

____

Who else needs to hear this quote today?

____

____

____

At the End of Your Day

How did I apply this quote today?

____

____

____

What will I do differently going forward?

____

____

____

"People say I make strange choices, but they're not strange for me. My sickness is that I'm fascinated by human behavior, by what's underneath the surface, by the worlds inside people." -Johnny Depp

Beginning Your Day

What does this quote mean to me personally today?

____
____
____

How will I apply this quote today?

____
____
____

Who else needs to hear this quote today?

____
____
____

At the End of Your Day

How did I apply this quote today?

____
____
____

What will I do differently going forward?

____
____
____

"Leadership is getting players to believe in you. If you tell a teammate you're ready to play as tough as you're able to, you'd better go out there and do it. Players will see right through a phony, and they can tell when you're not giving it all you've got." -Larry Bird

Beginning Your Day

What does this quote mean to me personally today?

____

____

____

How will I apply this quote today?

____

____

____

Who else needs to hear this quote today?

____

____

____

At the End of Your Day

How did I apply this quote today?

____

____

____

What will I do differently going forward?

____

____

____

"When saying 'yes' to others, make sure you aren't saying 'no' to yourself." -Paulo Coehlo

Beginning Your Day

What does this quote mean to me personally today?

____

____

____

How will I apply this quote today?

____

____

____

Who else needs to hear this quote today?

____

____

____

At the End of Your Day

How did I apply this quote today?

____

____

____

What will I do differently going forward?

____

____

____

"I attribute my success to this: I never gave or took any excuse." -Florence Nightingale

Beginning Your Day

What does this quote mean to me personally today?

____

____

____

How will I apply this quote today?

____

____

____

Who else needs to hear this quote today?

____

____

____

At the End of Your Day

How did I apply this quote today?

____

____

____

What will I do differently going forward?

____

____

____

"I can't change the direction of the wind, but I can adjust my sails to always reach my destination." -Jimmy Dean

Beginning Your Day

What does this quote mean to me personally today?

____

____

____

How will I apply this quote today?

____

____

____

Who else needs to hear this quote today?

____

____

____

At the End of Your Day

How did I apply this quote today?

____

____

____

What will I do differently going forward?

____

____

____

"Strong minds discuss ideas, average minds discuss events, weak minds discuss people." -Socrates

Beginning Your Day

What does this quote mean to me personally today?

____

____

____

How will I apply this quote today?

____

____

____

Who else needs to hear this quote today?

____

____

____

At the End of Your Day

How did I apply this quote today?

____

____

____

What will I do differently going forward?

____

____

____

"Let us always meet each other with a smile, for the smile is the beginning of love." -Mother Teresa

Beginning Your Day

What does this quote mean to me personally today?

____

____

____

How will I apply this quote today?

____

____

____

Who else needs to hear this quote today?

____

____

____

At the End of Your Day

How did I apply this quote today?

____

____

____

What will I do differently going forward?

____

____

____

"Tell me and I forget. Teach me and I remember. Involve me and I learn." -Benjamin Franklin

Beginning Your Day

What does this quote mean to me personally today?

____

____

____

How will I apply this quote today?

____

____

____

Who else needs to hear this quote today?

____

____

____

At the End of Your Day

How did I apply this quote today?

____

____

____

What will I do differently going forward?

____

____

____

"Your journey has molded you for your greater good, and it was exactly what it needed to be. Don't think that you've lost time. It took each and every situation you have encountered to bring you to the now. And now is right on time." -Asha Tyson

Beginning Your Day

What does this quote mean to me personally today?

____

____

____

How will I apply this quote today?

____

____

____

Who else needs to hear this quote today?

____

____

____

At the End of Your Day

How did I apply this quote today?

____

____

____

What will I do differently going forward?

____

____

____

"A smile is an inexpensive way to change your looks." -Charles Gordy

Beginning Your Day

What does this quote mean to me personally today?

____

____

____

How will I apply this quote today?

____

____

____

Who else needs to hear this quote today?

____

____

____

At the End of Your Day

How did I apply this quote today?

____

____

____

What will I do differently going forward?

____

____

____

"You can't have a better tomorrow if you are always thinking about yesterday." -Charles F. Kettering

Beginning Your Day

What does this quote mean to me personally today?

____

____

____

How will I apply this quote today?

____

____

____

Who else needs to hear this quote today?

____

____

____

At the End of Your Day

How did I apply this quote today?

____

____

____

What will I do differently going forward?

____

____

____

"Be grateful for what you have and stop complaining. It bores everyone else, does you no good, and doesn't solve any problems." -Zig Ziglar

Beginning Your Day

What does this quote mean to me personally today?

____

____

____

How will I apply this quote today?

____

____

____

Who else needs to hear this quote today?

____

____

____

At the End of Your Day

How did I apply this quote today?

____

____

____

What will I do differently going forward?

____

____

____

"Live as if you were to die tomorrow. Learn as if you were to live forever." -Mahatma Gandhi

Beginning Your Day

What does this quote mean to me personally today?

How will I apply this quote today?

Who else needs to hear this quote today?

At the End of Your Day

How did I apply this quote today?

What will I do differently going forward?

"When you share your experiences with other people, you take away their fears." -Rick Warren

Beginning Your Day

What does this quote mean to me personally today?

____

____

____

How will I apply this quote today?

____

____

____

Who else needs to hear this quote today?

____

____

____

At the End of Your Day

How did I apply this quote today?

____

____

____

What will I do differently going forward?

____

____

____

"If it scares you, it might be a good thing to try."
-Seth Godin

Beginning Your Day

What does this quote mean to me personally today?

____

____

____

How will I apply this quote today?

____

____

____

Who else needs to hear this quote today?

____

____

____

At the End of Your Day

How did I apply this quote today?

____

____

____

What will I do differently going forward?

____

____

____

"The measure of who we are is what we do with what we have." -Vince Lombardi

Beginning Your Day

What does this quote mean to me personally today?

____

____

____

How will I apply this quote today?

____

____

____

Who else needs to hear this quote today?

____

____

____

At the End of Your Day

How did I apply this quote today?

____

____

____

What will I do differently going forward?

____

____

____

"If you're able to be yourself, then you have no competition." -Barbra Cook

Beginning Your Day

What does this quote mean to me personally today?

____

____

____

How will I apply this quote today?

____

____

____

Who else needs to hear this quote today?

____

____

____

At the End of Your Day

How did I apply this quote today?

____

____

____

What will I do differently going forward?

____

____

____

"Strive not to be a success, but rather to be of value." -Albert Einstein

Beginning Your Day

What does this quote mean to me personally today?

____

____

____

How will I apply this quote today?

____

____

____

Who else needs to hear this quote today?

____

____

____

At the End of Your Day

How did I apply this quote today?

____

____

____

What will I do differently going forward?

____

____

____

"There is little success where there is little laughter." -Andrew Carnegie

Beginning Your Day

What does this quote mean to me personally today?

____

____

____

How will I apply this quote today?

____

____

____

Who else needs to hear this quote today?

____

____

____

At the End of Your Day

How did I apply this quote today?

____

____

____

What will I do differently going forward?

____

____

____

"If you hear a voice within you say 'you cannot paint,' then by all means, paint, and that voice will be silenced." -Vincent Van Gogh

Beginning Your Day

What does this quote mean to me personally today?

____

____

____

How will I apply this quote today?

____

____

____

Who else needs to hear this quote today?

____

____

____

At the End of Your Day

How did I apply this quote today?

____

____

____

What will I do differently going forward?

____

____

____

"Money and success don't change people; they merely amplify what is already there." -Will Smith

Beginning Your Day

What does this quote mean to me personally today?

____

____

____

How will I apply this quote today?

____

____

____

Who else needs to hear this quote today?

____

____

____

At the End of Your Day

How did I apply this quote today?

____

____

____

What will I do differently going forward?

____

____

____

"I'd rather regret the things I've done, than regret the things I haven't done." -Lucille Ball

Beginning Your Day

What does this quote mean to me personally today?

____

____

____

How will I apply this quote today?

____

____

____

Who else needs to hear this quote today?

____

____

____

At the End of Your Day

How did I apply this quote today?

____

____

____

What will I do differently going forward?

____

____

____

"Don't let the fear of striking out hold you back." -Babe Ruth

Beginning Your Day

What does this quote mean to me personally today?

____

____

____

How will I apply this quote today?

____

____

____

Who else needs to hear this quote today?

____

____

____

At the End of Your Day

How did I apply this quote today?

____

____

____

What will I do differently going forward?

____

____

____

"Listen to the mustn'ts, child. Listen to the don'ts. Listen to the shouldn'ts, the impossibles, the won'ts. Listen to the never haves, THEN listen close to me? Anything can happen, child. Anything can be." -Shel Silverstein

Beginning Your Day

What does this quote mean to me personally today?

____

____

____

How will I apply this quote today?

____

____

____

Who else needs to hear this quote today?

____

____

____

At the End of Your Day

How did I apply this quote today?

____

____

____

What will I do differently going forward?

____

____

____

"Happiness is not something you postpone for the future; it is something you design for the present." -Jim Rohn

Beginning Your Day

What does this quote mean to me personally today?

How will I apply this quote today?

Who else needs to hear this quote today?

At the End of Your Day

How did I apply this quote today?

What will I do differently going forward?

"Never make someone a priority when all you are to them is an option." -Maya Angelou

Beginning Your Day

What does this quote mean to me personally today?

____

____

____

How will I apply this quote today?

____

____

____

Who else needs to hear this quote today?

____

____

____

At the End of Your Day

How did I apply this quote today?

____

____

____

What will I do differently going forward?

____

____

____

"The only way to permanently change the temperature in the room is to reset the thermostat. In the same way, the only way to change your level of financial success 'permanently' is to reset your financial thermostat. But it is your choice whether you choose to change." -T. Harv Eker

Beginning Your Day

What does this quote mean to me personally today?

____

____

____

How will I apply this quote today?

____

____

____

Who else needs to hear this quote today?

____

____

____

At the End of Your Day

How did I apply this quote today?

____

____

____

What will I do differently going forward?

____

____

____

"Be yourself; everyone else is already taken."
-Oscar Wilde

Beginning Your Day

What does this quote mean to me personally today?

____

____

____

How will I apply this quote today?

____

____

____

Who else needs to hear this quote today?

____

____

____

At the End of Your Day

How did I apply this quote today?

____

____

____

What will I do differently going forward?

____

____

____

"A successful man will profit from his mistakes and try again in a different way." -Dale Carnegie

Beginning Your Day

What does this quote mean to me personally today?

____

____

____

How will I apply this quote today?

____

____

____

Who else needs to hear this quote today?

____

____

____

At the End of Your Day

How did I apply this quote today?

____

____

____

What will I do differently going forward?

____

____

____

"Communication is a skill that you can learn. It's like riding a bicycle or typing. If you're willing to work at it, you can rapidly improve the quality of every part of your life." -Brian Tracy

Beginning Your Day

What does this quote mean to me personally today?

____

____

____

How will I apply this quote today?

____

____

____

Who else needs to hear this quote today?

____

____

____

At the End of Your Day

How did I apply this quote today?

____

____

____

What will I do differently going forward?

____

____

____

"I do not fix problems. I fix my thinking. The problems fix themselves." -Louise Hay

Beginning Your Day

What does this quote mean to me personally today?

____

____

____

How will I apply this quote today?

____

____

____

Who else needs to hear this quote today?

____

____

____

At the End of Your Day

How did I apply this quote today?

____

____

____

What will I do differently going forward?

____

____

____

"Progress is impossible without change, and those who cannot change their minds cannot change anything." -George Bernard Shaw

Beginning Your Day

What does this quote mean to me personally today?

____

____

____

How will I apply this quote today?

____

____

____

Who else needs to hear this quote today?

____

____

____

At the End of Your Day

How did I apply this quote today?

____

____

____

What will I do differently going forward?

____

____

____

"Life is a series of experiences, each one of which makes us bigger, even though sometimes it is hard to realize this. For the world was built to develop character, and we must learn that the setbacks and grieves which we endure help us in our marching onward." -Henry Ford

Beginning Your Day

What does this quote mean to me personally today?

How will I apply this quote today?

Who else needs to hear this quote today?

At the End of Your Day

How did I apply this quote today?

What will I do differently going forward?

"Time is the most valuable thing you have; be sure to spend it well." -Lyndon Johnson

Beginning Your Day

What does this quote mean to me personally today?

____

____

____

How will I apply this quote today?

____

____

____

Who else needs to hear this quote today?

____

____

____

At the End of Your Day

How did I apply this quote today?

____

____

____

What will I do differently going forward?

____

____

____

"I believe the world is one big family, and we need to help each other." -Jet Li

Beginning Your Day

What does this quote mean to me personally today?

How will I apply this quote today?

Who else needs to hear this quote today?

At the End of Your Day

How did I apply this quote today?

What will I do differently going forward?

"Sometimes if you want to see a change for the better, you have to take things into your own hands." -Clint Eastwood

Beginning Your Day

What does this quote mean to me personally today?

____

____

____

How will I apply this quote today?

____

____

____

Who else needs to hear this quote today?

____

____

____

At the End of Your Day

How did I apply this quote today?

____

____

____

What will I do differently going forward?

____

____

____

"Nothing is impossible, the word itself says 'I'm possible'!" -Audrey Hepburn

Beginning Your Day

What does this quote mean to me personally today?

How will I apply this quote today?

Who else needs to hear this quote today?

At the End of Your Day

How did I apply this quote today?

What will I do differently going forward?

"The beginning is the most important part of the work." -Plato

Beginning Your Day

What does this quote mean to me personally today?

____
____
____

How will I apply this quote today?

____
____
____

Who else needs to hear this quote today?

____
____
____

At the End of Your Day

How did I apply this quote today?

____
____
____

What will I do differently going forward?

____
____
____

"If your actions inspire others to dream more, learn more, do more and become more, you are a leader." -John Quincy Adams

Beginning Your Day

What does this quote mean to me personally today?

____
____
____

How will I apply this quote today?

____
____
____

Who else needs to hear this quote today?

____
____
____

At the End of Your Day

How did I apply this quote today?

____
____
____

What will I do differently going forward?

____
____
____

"I think that music in itself is healing. It's an explosive expression of humanity. It's something we are all touched by. No matter what culture we're from, everyone loves music." -Billy Joel

Beginning Your Day

What does this quote mean to me personally today?

How will I apply this quote today?

Who else needs to hear this quote today?

At the End of Your Day

How did I apply this quote today?

What will I do differently going forward?

"I have found the paradox, that if you love until it hurts, there can be no more hurt, only more love." -Mother Teresa

Beginning Your Day

What does this quote mean to me personally today?

____

____

____

How will I apply this quote today?

____

____

____

Who else needs to hear this quote today?

____

____

____

At the End of Your Day

How did I apply this quote today?

____

____

____

What will I do differently going forward?

____

____

____

"Integrity is everything. With it, you can weather all storms. Without it, even little things will derail you. Hold true to your commitments because relationships are either built or undone by them."
-Michael Stevenson

Beginning Your Day
What does this quote mean to me personally today?

____

____

____

How will I apply this quote today?

____

____

____

Who else needs to hear this quote today?

____

____

____

At the End of Your Day
How did I apply this quote today?

____

____

____

What will I do differently going forward?

____

____

____

"Mystery creates wonder and wonder is the basis of man's desire to understand." -Neil Armstrong

Beginning Your Day

What does this quote mean to me personally today?

How will I apply this quote today?

Who else needs to hear this quote today?

At the End of Your Day

How did I apply this quote today?

What will I do differently going forward?

"In wisdom gathered over time I have found that every experience is a form of exploration." -Ansel Adams

Beginning Your Day

What does this quote mean to me personally today?

____

____

____

How will I apply this quote today?

____

____

____

Who else needs to hear this quote today?

____

____

____

At the End of Your Day

How did I apply this quote today?

____

____

____

What will I do differently going forward?

____

____

____

"The size of your success is measured by the strength of your desire; the size of your dream; and how you handle disappointment along the way." -Robert Kiyosaki

Beginning Your Day

What does this quote mean to me personally today?

How will I apply this quote today?

Who else needs to hear this quote today?

At the End of Your Day

How did I apply this quote today?

What will I do differently going forward?

"I am only one, but, I am one. I cannot do everything, but, I can do something, and I will not let what I cannot do interfere with what I can do."
-Edward Everett Hale

Beginning Your Day

What does this quote mean to me personally today?

____

____

How will I apply this quote today?

____

____

Who else needs to hear this quote today?

____

____

At the End of Your Day

How did I apply this quote today?

____

____

What will I do differently going forward?

____

____

"If God can use a man without arms and legs to be His hands and feet, then He will certainly use any willing heart!" -Nick Vujicic

Beginning Your Day

What does this quote mean to me personally today?

____

____

How will I apply this quote today?

____

____

____

Who else needs to hear this quote today?

____

____

At the End of Your Day

How did I apply this quote today?

____

____

What will I do differently going forward?

____

____

____

"Never mistake motion for action." -Ernest Hemingway

Beginning Your Day

What does this quote mean to me personally today?

____

____

____

How will I apply this quote today?

____

____

____

Who else needs to hear this quote today?

____

____

____

At the End of Your Day

How did I apply this quote today?

____

____

____

What will I do differently going forward?

____

____

____

**"What is success? I think it is a mixture of having a flair for the thing that you are doing; knowing that it is not enough, that you have got to have hard work and a certain sense of purpose."
-Margaret Thatcher**

Beginning Your Day
What does this quote mean to me personally today?

____
____
____

How will I apply this quote today?

____
____
____

Who else needs to hear this quote today?

____
____
____

At the End of Your Day
How did I apply this quote today?

____
____
____

What will I do differently going forward?

____
____
____

"I don't believe in circumstances. The people who get on in this world are the people who get up and look for the circumstances they want, and, if they can't find them, make them." -George Bernard Shaw

Beginning Your Day

What does this quote mean to me personally today?

____

____

____

How will I apply this quote today?

____

____

____

Who else needs to hear this quote today?

____

____

____

At the End of Your Day

How did I apply this quote today?

____

____

____

What will I do differently going forward?

____

____

____

"It is better to lead from behind and to put others in front, especially when you celebrate victory when nice things occur. You take the front line when there is danger. Then people will appreciate your leadership." -Nelson Mandela

Beginning Your Day
What does this quote mean to me personally today?

____
____
____

How will I apply this quote today?

____
____
____

Who else needs to hear this quote today?

____
____
____

At the End of Your Day
How did I apply this quote today?

____
____
____

What will I do differently going forward?

____
____
____

"We can learn something new anytime we believe we can." -Virginia Satir

Beginning Your Day

What does this quote mean to me personally today?

How will I apply this quote today?

Who else needs to hear this quote today?

At the End of Your Day

How did I apply this quote today?

What will I do differently going forward?

"A wise man can learn more from a foolish question than a fool can learn from a wise answer." -Bruce Lee

Beginning Your Day

What does this quote mean to me personally today?

How will I apply this quote today?

Who else needs to hear this quote today?

At the End of Your Day

How did I apply this quote today?

What will I do differently going forward?

"Experience has shown, and a true philosophy will always show, that a vast, perhaps the larger portion of the truth arises from the seemingly irrelevant." -Edgar Allan Poe

Beginning Your Day

What does this quote mean to me personally today?

____

____

____

How will I apply this quote today?

____

____

____

Who else needs to hear this quote today?

____

____

____

At the End of Your Day

How did I apply this quote today?

____

____

____

What will I do differently going forward?

____

____

____

"As long as we persevere and endure, we can get anything we want." -Mike Tyson

Beginning Your Day
What does this quote mean to me personally today?

____

____

____

How will I apply this quote today?

____

____

____

Who else needs to hear this quote today?

____

____

____

At the End of Your Day
How did I apply this quote today?

____

____

____

What will I do differently going forward?

____

____

____

"To effectively communicate, we must realize that we are all different in the way we perceive the world and use this understanding as a guide to our communication with others." -Tony Robbins

Beginning Your Day

What does this quote mean to me personally today?

____

____

____

How will I apply this quote today?

____

____

____

Who else needs to hear this quote today?

____

____

____

At the End of Your Day

How did I apply this quote today?

____

____

____

What will I do differently going forward?

____

____

____

"Don't find fault, find a remedy." -Henry Ford

Beginning Your Day

What does this quote mean to me personally today?

____

____

____

How will I apply this quote today?

____

____

____

Who else needs to hear this quote today?

____

____

____

At the End of Your Day

How did I apply this quote today?

____

____

____

What will I do differently going forward?

____

____

____

"Your smile will give you a positive countenance that will make people feel comfortable around you." -Les Brown

Beginning Your Day

What does this quote mean to me personally today?

____

____

____

How will I apply this quote today?

____

____

____

Who else needs to hear this quote today?

____

____

____

At the End of Your Day

How did I apply this quote today?

____

____

____

What will I do differently going forward?

____

____

____

"Do the one thing you think you cannot do. Fail at it. Try again. Do better the second time. The only people who never tumble are those who never mount the high wire. This is your moment. Own it." -Oprah Winfrey

Beginning Your Day

What does this quote mean to me personally today?

How will I apply this quote today?

Who else needs to hear this quote today?

At the End of Your Day

How did I apply this quote today?

What will I do differently going forward?

"Open your eyes, look within. Are you satisfied with the life you're living?" -Bob Marley

Beginning Your Day

What does this quote mean to me personally today?

How will I apply this quote today?

Who else needs to hear this quote today?

At the End of Your Day

How did I apply this quote today?

What will I do differently going forward?

"See Beauty,
Give Grace,
Speak Life,
Live Loved." -Natasha Bryant- Poet

Beginning Your Day

What does this quote mean to me personally today?

____
____
____

How will I apply this quote today?

____
____
____

Who else needs to hear this quote today?

____
____
____

At the End of Your Day

How did I apply this quote today?

____
____
____

What will I do differently going forward?

____
____
____

"Our greatest weakness lies in giving up. The most certain way to succeed is always to try just one more time." -Thomas A. Edison

Beginning Your Day

What does this quote mean to me personally today?

____

____

____

How will I apply this quote today?

____

____

____

Who else needs to hear this quote today?

____

____

____

At the End of Your Day

How did I apply this quote today?

____

____

____

What will I do differently going forward?

____

____

____

"Keep your face to the sunshine and you cannot see a shadow." -Helen Keller

Beginning Your Day

What does this quote mean to me personally today?

How will I apply this quote today?

Who else needs to hear this quote today?

At the End of Your Day

How did I apply this quote today?

What will I do differently going forward?

"I have learned over the years that when one's mind is made up, that diminishes fear; knowing what must be done does away with fear." -Rosa Parks

Beginning Your Day

What does this quote mean to me personally today?

____

____

How will I apply this quote today?

____

____

Who else needs to hear this quote today?

____

____

At the End of Your Day

How did I apply this quote today?

____

____

What will I do differently going forward?

____

____

"Always put your best self forward, and keep a smile on your face, because you never know when someone is being encouraged by, or falling in love with your smile." -Kayla Moffett Stevenson

Beginning Your Day

What does this quote mean to me personally today?

____

____

____

How will I apply this quote today?

____

____

____

Who else needs to hear this quote today?

____

____

____

At the End of Your Day

How did I apply this quote today?

____

____

____

What will I do differently going forward?

____

____

____

"If you can dream it, you can do it." -Walt Disney

Beginning Your Day

What does this quote mean to me personally today?

____

____

____

How will I apply this quote today?

____

____

____

Who else needs to hear this quote today?

____

____

____

At the End of Your Day

How did I apply this quote today?

____

____

____

What will I do differently going forward?

____

____

____

"The starting point of all achievement is desire." -Napoleon Hill

Beginning Your Day

What does this quote mean to me personally today?

____

____

____

How will I apply this quote today?

____

____

____

Who else needs to hear this quote today?

____

____

____

At the End of Your Day

How did I apply this quote today?

____

____

____

What will I do differently going forward?

____

____

____

"Any man who reads too much and uses his own brain too little falls into lazy habits of thinking."
-Albert Einstein

Beginning Your Day

What does this quote mean to me personally today?

____

____

____

How will I apply this quote today?

____

____

____

Who else needs to hear this quote today?

____

____

____

At the End of Your Day

How did I apply this quote today?

____

____

____

What will I do differently going forward?

____

____

____

"If you are the kind of person who is waiting for the 'right' thing to happen, you might wait for a long time. It's like waiting for all the traffic lights to be green for five miles before starting the trip."
-Robert Kiyosaki

Beginning Your Day
What does this quote mean to me personally today?

____

____

____

How will I apply this quote today?

____

____

____

Who else needs to hear this quote today?

____

____

____

At the End of Your Day
How did I apply this quote today?

____

____

____

What will I do differently going forward?

____

____

____

"If we are not a little bit uncomfortable every day, we're not growing. All the good stuff is outside our comfort zone." -Jack Canfield

Beginning Your Day

What does this quote mean to me personally today?

____

____

____

How will I apply this quote today?

____

____

____

Who else needs to hear this quote today?

____

____

____

At the End of Your Day

How did I apply this quote today?

____

____

____

What will I do differently going forward?

____

____

____

"The Constitution only gives people the right to pursue happiness. You have to catch it yourself." -Benjamin Franklin

Beginning Your Day

What does this quote mean to me personally today?

____

____

____

How will I apply this quote today?

____

____

____

Who else needs to hear this quote today?

____

____

____

At the End of Your Day

How did I apply this quote today?

____

____

____

What will I do differently going forward?

____

____

____

"Darkness cannot drive out darkness; only light can do that. Hate cannot drive out hate; only love can do that." -Martin Luther King, Jr.

Beginning Your Day

What does this quote mean to me personally today?

____

____

____

How will I apply this quote today?

____

____

____

Who else needs to hear this quote today?

____

____

____

At the End of Your Day

How did I apply this quote today?

____

____

____

What will I do differently going forward?

____

____

____

"Your attitude is either the lock on or key to your door of success." -Denis Waitley

Beginning Your Day

What does this quote mean to me personally today?

How will I apply this quote today?

Who else needs to hear this quote today?

At the End of Your Day

How did I apply this quote today?

What will I do differently going forward?

"Trust is the glue of life. It's the most essential ingredient in effective communication. It's the foundational principle that holds all relationships." -Stephen Covey

Beginning Your Day

What does this quote mean to me personally today?

____

____

____

How will I apply this quote today?

____

____

____

Who else needs to hear this quote today?

____

____

____

At the End of Your Day

How did I apply this quote today?

____

____

____

What will I do differently going forward?

____

____

____

"I am always doing that which I cannot do, in order that I may learn how to do it." -Pablo Picasso

Beginning Your Day

What does this quote mean to me personally today?

____

____

____

How will I apply this quote today?

____

____

____

Who else needs to hear this quote today?

____

____

____

At the End of Your Day

How did I apply this quote today?

____

____

____

What will I do differently going forward?

____

____

____

"I believe that through knowledge and discipline, financial peace is possible for all of us." -Dave Ramsey

Beginning Your Day

What does this quote mean to me personally today?

____

____

____

How will I apply this quote today?

____

____

____

Who else needs to hear this quote today?

____

____

____

At the End of Your Day

How did I apply this quote today?

____

____

____

What will I do differently going forward?

____

____

____

"Hardships often prepare ordinary people for an extraordinary destiny." -C.S. Lewis

Beginning Your Day

What does this quote mean to me personally today?

____

____

____

How will I apply this quote today?

____

____

____

Who else needs to hear this quote today?

____

____

____

At the End of Your Day

How did I apply this quote today?

____

____

____

What will I do differently going forward?

____

____

____

"I like to listen. I have learned a great deal from listening carefully. Most people never listen."
-Ernest Hemingway

Beginning Your Day

What does this quote mean to me personally today?

____

____

____

How will I apply this quote today?

____

____

____

Who else needs to hear this quote today?

____

____

____

At the End of Your Day

How did I apply this quote today?

____

____

____

What will I do differently going forward?

____

____

____

"When I was 5 years old, my mother always told me that happiness was the key to life. When I went to school, they asked me what I wanted to be when I grew up. I wrote down 'happy'. They told me that I didn't understand the assignment, and I told them they didn't understand life." -John Lennon

Beginning Your Day
What does this quote mean to me personally today?

____

____

____

How will I apply this quote today?

____

____

____

Who else needs to hear this quote today?

____

____

____

At the End of Your Day
How did I apply this quote today?

____

____

____

What will I do differently going forward?

____

____

____

"Here's to the crazy ones, the misfits, the rebels, the troublemakers, the round pegs in the square holes, the ones who see things differently. They're not fond of rules. You can quote them, disagree with them, glorify or vilify them, but the only thing you can't do is ignore them because they change things? The ones who are crazy enough to think that they can change the world, are the ones who do." -Steve Jobs

Beginning Your Day
What does this quote mean to me personally today?

____

____

____

How will I apply this quote today?

____

____

____

Who else needs to hear this quote today?

____

____

____

At the End of Your Day
How did I apply this quote today?

____

____

____

What will I do differently going forward?

____

____

____

"You were not put here to live a mediocre life. You were put here to shine." -Michael Stevenson

Beginning Your Day

What does this quote mean to me personally today?

____

____

____

How will I apply this quote today?

____

____

____

Who else needs to hear this quote today?

____

____

____

At the End of Your Day

How did I apply this quote today?

____

____

____

What will I do differently going forward?

____

____

____

www.ingramcontent.com/pod-product-compliance
Lightning Source LLC
Chambersburg PA
CBHW070815240726
48654CB00007B/356